the drummer's almanac

WRITTEN BY JON COHAN

ISBN 0-7935-6696-7

HAL•LEONARD®
CORPORATION
7777 W. BLUEMOUND RD. P.O. BOX 13819 MILWAUKEE, WI 53213

Visit Hal Leonard Online at
www.halleonard.com

table of contents

Did you hear about the guitarist who was on his way to a gig and locked his keys in the car?   It took him two hours to get the drummer out.

Photo by Sarah Beth Wiley

Jon Cohan

introduction

To be a drummer is to be misunderstood. That old joke about the band consisting of three musicians and a drummer reflects the uninformed view of many people who still see the drummer as a barbarian with a haircut, making indiscriminate noise. It is a noble and often thankless endeavor - at the simplest level, we are there to keep time. The pulse is the foundation upon which all music is built. We supply the groove, the feel, the swing, the heartbeat, the rhythm that moves the music. It's arguably the most important job in the band. As the saying goes, a bad drummer can make a great band sound awful, but a good drummer can make a bad group sound great. At it's best, drumming transcends timekeeping and heightens the experience of the music, the musicians, and the listeners.

My idea for the Drummers Almanac started out as a simple interest in speaking to a handful of drummers about their lives as musicians - how they got started, their first big break, what inspires them, etc. I wanted to represent a range of drum set players who were both successful and influential in their chosen area of music. Over the course of the interviews, I noticed a common thread which tied together the diverse narratives of these different people. All the drummers shared a deep and immovable belief in their art, and an unshakable and tireless enthusiasm for their music. This seems to me to be the key to success in any profession. I'd like to thank these drummers for their help and inspiration - it is to them that I dedicate this book.

Jon Cohan November 1997

Acknowledgements

Many grateful thanks to Brad Smith at Hal Leonard for his encouragement, his ideas, and his thoughtful goading. Thanks to Steve Anzivino at Yamaha for his help in facilitating interviews. Also thanks to: Leila Cohan, Leon and Heidi Cohan, Mimi Rapp, Diane Gershuny, Mark and Cindy Lammie, LSlashL Design, Noelle Ciocchetti, Craig Schuman, Centre Street Drums, Andy Doerschuk, Frank Briggs, Chris Parker, Dave Weckl, Peter Erskine, Terri Lyne Carrington, Fred Buda, Anton Fig, Carter Beauford, Andy Newmark, Alex Acuña, Rick VanHorn, Nanette Lorenz, Manny Wise, Colin Schofield, Jon Eiche, John Aldridge, John King, Rick Roccapriore, Andy Pinkham, Mortal Music Studios, Tom Brechtlein, and The Percussive Arts Society.

Alex Acuña

Courtesy of Yamaha

about drumming

ANTON FIG:

I always felt like the drums chose me, not the other way around. I remember my parents bringing back some drumsticks and brushes. That was because I used to play on pots and pans. Then a friend of my parents bought me a toy set when I was five. I remember being led downstairs with a blindfold on to this set of drums — it had cloth heads. When I was six, my grandfather bought me a snare and bass drum. Every year he would add a drum. By the time I was ten, I had a full kit, and I've been gigging ever since.

Alex Acuña and the Unknowns,
Weather Report,
Koinonia,
Antonio Carlos Jobim,
The Yellowjackets

ALEX ACUÑA:

I come from a very poor family, and we didn't have any money to buy instruments, so my father made some drums. He bought secondhand drums and rebuilt them, and he killed the sheep to make the drumhead. So I had a big bass drum, a snare, and a timbale, with a cowbell, one hi-hat, and one cymbal; that was my setup when I was eleven years old. The cowbell was mounted on a little pillow on top the bass drum—no toms at all. Everything was homemade. Out of little barrels, my father made congas and bongos.

Then there's the one about the bassist who was so out of tune the band actually noticed.

CARTER BEAUFORD:

My father, who was a trumpet player, was my first inspiration. He had a band (I was two or three years old at the time), and the drummer in his band, Mike Satterfield, was really cool—beret and all that. I used to watch him. Then my dad took me to see a Buddy Rich concert, and that totally blew me away. That got me started—planted the whole seed. My dad's thing, being a musician, was to expose his kids to music, and I'm glad he did.

From there I got into different drummers, and by doing that learned about different musicians: sax players, guitar players, bass players. So it opened up a brand new thing for me, something that just swept me away and made me get into music heavily. It took me by storm the first day, and it's been that way ever since. It's even getting stronger! I knew I was gonna be a drummer when I was three years old. People say, "How could you know?" Believe me, I knew!

DAVE WECKL:

The first memory of drumming for me was setting up cardboard boxes and pot lids on my bed and playing to records. I had actually started playing guitar, taking lessons, and just didn't dig it. The people next door had three kids that had a family rock band. My parents were always into music, mostly jazz stuff, and there was always something going on. My dad was an amateur piano player. I was always drawn to music, performance, and sports. I figured out pretty quickly guitar was too difficult and I didn't really have the interest to do it. My dad saw my interest in drums, because I had banged up enough of my mom's pot lids. They got me a cheap little drum set that I could play to records with. I did that for three or four years and got a real drum set.

TERRI LYNE CARRINGTON:

My grandfather's drums were in the house; he played, but he passed away before I was born. I would ask my father to set them up so I could play. My father was a saxophone player, but he started out playing drums, so he knew enough to show me basic stuff, and I would also play along with records. It was something fun to do, and after a couple of years I started playing gigs. I played my first professional gig when I was ten. At that point I never thought of doing anything else. By the time I was a teenager, I couldn't remember not playing drums. It just seemed a natural part of my life.

Carter Beauford

Courtesy of Yamaha

PAUL LEIM:

I grew up in East Texas. I was the drum section leader in the high school band when I was in eighth grade. Small school—there was only thirty-six kids in our entire graduating class. The high school band consisted of the high school and junior high band in order to have enough kids. We had a great band, we won a lot of contests. We also had your typical high school rock and roll bands playing Beatles songs and Buckingham songs. I always loved pop music. Our band worked every night, so we had to play what was popular. In retrospect, when you grow up listening and playing all that, you learn what's needed in a song.

Courtesy of Yamaha

CARTER BEAUFORD:

My dad bought me a little tin-rimmed kit with the paper heads, and I held on to that for about a month. I would stretch towels over the rims and pretend I was the drummer in my dad's band or Buddy Rich. That's what I wanted to do; I fell in love with the whole idea of drumming.

My brothers and I would go up to this park and see these bands play, and I would be right behind the drummer the whole time, studying his every move. I still think that's one of the best ways to learn your craft—to see these guys perform and create on their instrument.

Dave Matthews Band
BET

ANDY NEWMARK:

Everybody at school was learning an instrument and I just picked out drums, I'm not sure why. It didn't even become fun till years after that, around seventh grade. I was hearing music I was digging for the first time. I saw the drums as a connection to that music and thought, "Oh, maybe this could be good."

8 *Why did the chicken cross the road?   To get away from the bass solo.*

Courtesy of Yamaha

FRED BUDA:

My mother and father used to take me to these Italian picnics, and they would always have bands there. They used to let me sit in, because I was playing on pots and pans at home.

I didn't have lessons when I was a kid; I taught myself to play. That's okay, because I learned to use my instincts. I started going to clubs and was playing in New Bedford [Massachusetts] with people like Paul Gonsalves [of Duke Ellington's band]. I taught myself to read. The way I taught myself was to be "almost right." It's like being "almost pregnant."

ANTON FIG:

My dad had a great jazz collection and my mom was into classical music, and I listened to a lot of African music. I grew up in Capetown [South Africa] with that music. You'd hear it on the radio all the time.

DAVE WECKL:

I would play with my dad, and he got me into different styles of music. The rock stuff was so easy for me to copy, the challenge of it went away. The jazz stuff was more difficult and interesting. It was a challenge to me to see if I could copy what was going on in the records.

Courtesy of John Aldridge

Super Ludwig Deluxe Outfit

A Short History of The Drum Set

FOR ALL ITS RELATIVE YOUTH, THE DRUM SET HAS QUICKLY
EVOLVED FROM A SOMEWHAT PRIMITIVE CONTRAPTION (SOME
SAY "CONTRAPTION" IS WHERE THE WORD "TRAPS" CAME
FROM) TO A HIGHLY ENGINEERED MUSICAL INSTRUMENT. BUT
DID YOU EVER STOP AND THINK HOW THIS CONGLOMERATION
OF STANDS, LUGS, AND SHELLS COME INTO BEING? IT'S
IMPORTANT TO RECOGNIZE THAT, WHILE THE DRUM SET
DIDN'T EXIST UNTIL ABOUT A HUNDRED YEARS AGO, THE
ACTUAL ART OF DRUMMING AS A MUSICAL SKILL HAD BEEN
DEVELOPING FOR THOUSANDS OF YEARS.

Drums and drumming have always been associated with rituals—the ritual of war, of birth, religion, death, and celebration. Military drumming itself served many purposes, not the least of which was to create a cadence, or beat, for marching soldiers. Even European classical music included parts written for snare drum, timpani, and cymbals. In Africa and Asia, drumming was, and is, a fundamental ingredient of everyday life. When Africans were taken from their homeland and forced into slavery

Courtesy of John Aldridge

Why do bands have bass players?   To translate for the drummer.

Super Ludwig Snare Drum, 1926

Chinese Tom Toms

Leedy Rollaway Console – predecessor of the modern rack system

in America and the West Indies, they tried to retain many of their traditions and beliefs, against great pressure to give them up. The hodgepodge of all these diverse musical traditions was nowhere more evident than in New Orleans, where music from Europe, Africa, and the Caribbean was thrown into the pot along with military and marching music, and the resulting gumbo eventually yielded jazz.

In the late 1800s, with New Orleans a bustling port city, the blend was potent and popular. Former slaves had combined African rhythmic syncopations with the popular European music and military marches, and they performed this mixture in clubs, riverboats, theaters, and bawdy houses. Instead of being parade bands, these were stationary groups, where the previously requisite snare drummer and bass drummer found themselves with much less room to work their magic. Because a band's major function was to provide music for dancers, the drums were the heartbeat of the group. Eventually it fell upon the drummer to perform more complicated rhythms than could be carried out on just the snare and bass drums; the drums now had to be consolidated, and other sounds needed to be added to punctuate the music.

The bass drum pedal was one of the first innovations to the new agglomeration. The early pedals were primitive shades of the hi-tech kick pedals we have nowadays—many were crude mechanical devices that served the dual purpose of bass drum beater and cymbal striker. As demand grew for an efficient pedal, many companies responded with products that were not too far removed from our modern pedals. Ultimately the cymbal striker arm on the bass drum pedal was replaced by the low boy, a shorter version of the later hi-hat, or sock, cymbal, which itself appeared on the drumming scene in the late 1920s.

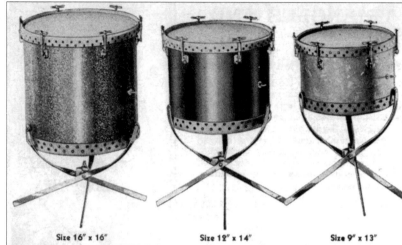

Pigskin Tom Toms from 1935 Ludwig Catalog

Size 16" x 16"   Size 12" x 14"   Size 9" x 13"

Courtesy of John Aldridge

Retro-modern cocktail drum by Yamaha

Photo by Jon Cohan

An early drum kit often consisted of a snare drum, a bass drum (usually 26" or larger!), a mounted cymbal or two, wood block(s), cowbell(s), and a tacked-head Chinese tom-tom. As vaudeville and, later, silent movies, grew in popularity, so did the drummer's responsibility. It wasn't unusual for drummers from the early 1900s to have a large number of sound effects in the orchestra pit (whistles, dog barks, birdcalls, car horns, etc.), along with their drums, cymbals, and other percussion.

Near the end of the 1920s, big band and swing music were beginning to create a great demand for quality and design among the major drum companies. Distinctive innovations, such as single-ply maple-shell snare drums, self-aligning lugs, more durable hardware, and colorful plastic

coverings, stimulated competition in the growing drum businesses. In Guide to Vintage Drums (Centerstream Publishing), drum expert John Aldridge cites Gene Krupa as popularizing the tom-tom with tunable top and bottom heads and the now-standard four-piece kit. By the mid 1930s, spurred on by the swing craze, companies like Slingerland, Ludwig, Leedy, and Gretsch were selling drums faster than they could build them.

During the big band era, many drum sets were just a variation on the four-piece theme, but drum companies strove to offer amenities to the consumer to set their products above the rest of the pack. Fanciful finishes, plating, and elaborate snare throw-offs and snare drum designs were common. You can even see the precursors of many of today's drum

12   *What's the difference between a trombone and a casket?   The casket has the corpse on the inside*

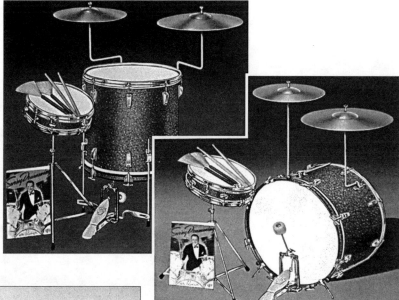

1950's WFL Kits

1950's Gretsch Jazz Kit

kit items in the products of the day, like the rolling console or trap table, which served about the same purpose as modern drum rack systems. When World War II broke out, many drum companies severely reduced their production due to government laws limiting the amount of metal used on a nonessential product to 10 percent of the total weight of the product. The drums made during that era featured ingenious wood lugs, hoops, and snare mechanisms, but many of the top lines were discontinued until after the war.

In the late forties, jazz turned from large bands to smaller groups playing bebop. The drummer's job changed: now instead of being just the pulse and timekeeper of the band, he or she had to rhythmically interact and underscore the new fast-paced compositions. Likewise, the sizes of drums started to change during this period, from the big 26" and 28" bass drums, 14" rack toms, and 16" floor toms, to more compact and transportable 18" and 20" bass drums, 12" mounted toms, 14" floor toms, and small 3x13" piccolo snare drums. Before the 1950s, when Mylar came into use as a dependable alternative, drumheads had been made of

Carter Beauford's drum kit – 1996

animal skins, most notably calfskin and pigskin.

The 1950s brought new affluence to the U.S., and with that a new music, rock and roll, which was born out of rhythm and blues and country music. Rock and roll fever swept the country much in the same way big band frenzy had twenty years before. The popularity of rock and roll and jazz, coupled with America's fascination with the "Atomic Age," was reflected in the drum designs of the day. Names like "Progressive," "Compacto," and "Dyna-Sonic" became the drum companies' space-age stock in trade.

In the 1960s, all hell broke loose with the British rock invasion, led by those four fab lads from Liverpool, The Beatles. The impact of The Beatles on the musical instrument industry was huge. While the Ludwig Drum Company most obviously benefited from Ringo's use of their drums, all the other companies shared in the increased sales. Along with "groovy" new finishes and setup styles, hardware became an area of competition for rival drum makers. Tom-tom mounts, lugs, and stands were made sturdier to accommodate the harder-hitting rock drummers. By the late sixties and early seventies, larger kits began showing up in drum catalogs and on stages, where the drummer had to compete for volume with amplified guitars and basses.

Drum recording techniques in the 1970s changed the design of drums. The practice of close-miking drums and the search for a deeper, less resonant sound caused many drum makers to offer kits with no bottom heads on the tom-toms or bass drums. Tom-toms were made in larger depths, and every effort was made to remove the ringing of the drums in the studio. Drum companies also started experimenting with different materials for shell construction—fiberglass, acrylic, and plastic composites were marketed with fair success. Ludwig even marketed a set, called the Tivoli, with rows of blinking lights built into

14 What did the drummer get on his I.Q. test?   Drool

Courtesy of Yamaha

the clear acrylic shells. It was during the seventies that foreign-built drums started making inroads into the American market. Along with the expanded competition came more innovations vying for the customer's attention. Since basic drum design hadn't changed much, the battle was again waged on the fronts of hardware, finish, and shell design. Systems for mounting large numbers of tom-toms and cymbals were developed, as were new conceptions of kick and hi-hat pedals.

The last decade or so has seen a shift back to traditional drum design, with a twist. Drum makers have taken familiar ideas, such as the cocktail drum, the tube lug, and the hand-hammered cymbal, and updated them with modern engineering. By paying respect to—and learning from—history, the traditions of the past continue to feed the invention of the future.

A short History of the Drum set ⑮

BY DAVE WECKL

Courtesy of Yamaha

Dave Weckl

A Natural Approach to Drumming

AS MUSICIANS STUDYING TO CONTINUOUSLY IMPROVE, WE ALL

GO THROUGH DIFFERENT PHASES IN OUR LIVES OF LEARNING

FROM TEACHERS, HEARING NEW MUSIC, HEARING OLD MUSIC,

CONSTANTLY PRACTICING, AND BEING AFFECTED BY THE

EVOLUTION OF ALL THINGS IN LIFE.

(*Dave is the author of* Contemporary Drummer + One). As of this writing, I've been playing drums for twenty-eight years, and recently started to study with a world-renowned teacher, Freddie Gruber. Freddie has spent his life analyzing some of the great jazz drummers of our time and has a real grasp on how the physiology of drumming works. His concepts and ideas have helped me reach a new level in my playing, and although there are many elements to his teachings, there are a couple of points that I think are important for a player at any level to know. Within the limited space allotted me here, I will briefly touch on them. I'm sure in the future Freddie will have all his ideas documented in some way.

The whole concept is to be able to play the drums with as little physical effort as possible—unless you want to work hard to play the instrument! The key word here is natural. The approach to holding the sticks, making a stroke, and obtaining the subsequent sound should be a very natural one. The body motion involved should coincide with the way the drummer's bones, muscles, and joints were designed to move.

How do you know when a drummer is at the door?   The knocking speeds up.

Photo by Jon Cohan

Without getting too technical, if you hit any surface with your hand, you would naturally strike it with your palm, like a conga player would. Notice this motion, then pick up a stick, and without thinking about a "grip," make the same motion to strike a surface, holding the stick as loose as possible. This is the beginning of thinking "naturally." Also, when you make the stroke, allow the stick to rebound as much as possible. This is the "action/reaction" concept that Freddie teaches. If you make a stroke and forcefully stop the stick close to the head with a tight grip, you're stopping the natural reaction of the stick. Not only will this make you work harder, but it will also choke the sound, because you're gripping the stick too tight. Too often drummers make the mistake of thinking that more physical strength and down force to the drums means more sound, which is only 50 percent correct. But without just as much thought going into the reaction, or rebound, the full amount of power and sound is not realized.

The other "natural" approach concept is very basic. You have to set up the drums in a position that will allow natural body movement. The first thing I did after my initial lesson with Freddie was tear down my set and start over, with the idea that everything had to be comfortable to hit. Don't be afraid to experiment with a setup that feels good and natural to you.

The end result of these concepts has made it easier and more enjoyable for me to play the drums. The music you make will feel and sound more relaxed, and have a nice loose quality, without the tension in your body caused by "unnatural" body motion. Give it a try; I'm sure you'll like it!

Photo by Jon Cohan

Photo by Jon Cohan

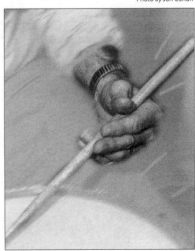

A Natural Approach to Drumming

about drumming

Sly and The Family Stone, John Lennon, Roxy Music, David Bowie, Roger Waters, Laura Nyro, Eric Clapton

ANDY NEWMARK:

I always felt that I had a point of view on my instrument, and it was that knowledge that helped me to go on and be successful. I always liked what was coming out. I always knew if I was playing like me or if I stepped over the line. I knew what kind of vibe I wanted to come off the drum set, and everything I did was toward that end. I had some idea of the way I wanted the drums to sound and feel.

ALEX ACUÑA:

My father is an excellent musician. He was self-taught, but he learned to play many instruments. We were six brothers and three sisters. My mother didn't want me to be a musician, because I was the youngest boy. My father didn't take much time teaching me. My brothers used to rehearse in the house, and I was there during the rehearsals, under the table or sitting in the corner, so I learned the tunes just by listening. And then one day (I was about ten years old), the drummer, who was one of my brothers, had another gig and couldn't make a gig, so I said, "I can play the tunes!" and they laughed. But I rehearsed with them, and they said, "How do you know all the tunes?" and I told them I listened in rehearsal. So they took me to the gig. I was only in fourth grade! Later on, my brothers taught me how to play the trumpet, so I was playing trumpet in a band, doubling on drums, from the age of twelve to sixteen.

Courtesy of Yamaha

Andy Newmark

What's the difference between a saxophone and a lawn mower?   The grip.

Courtesy of Yamaha

When I became sixteen, I went to Lima. My brothers were already set up there as studio musicians, and they recommended me. They set me up, and I immediately started recording for Odeon. I became the staff drummer and started doing TV work and nightclubs. I was working from nine o'clock in the morning to three o'clock in the morning when I was eighteen.

CARTER BEAUFORD:

My first paying gig, I was nine years old, playing with a group called the Morgan White Band. Morgan White wasn't the name of anyone in the band, it was just a name they thought would sell. The music was almost like fusion. I gigged enough that I was the richest nine-year-old on the block. I was always practicing, and the neighbors would complain all the time, calling the police on me. I was terrified of the police!

PAUL LEIM:

We were playing a city park in Tyler, Texas, called Bergfeld Park. This studio owner named Robin Hood Bryants came up to me (I was fifteen years old), and said, "Kid, you got a metronome in your head. How'd you like to work in the studio?" So I went in and I started immediately making records when I was fifteen years old. We did records and Dairy Queen commercials and Exxon commercials. It was a really busy studio. Most of the stuff was on a label out of Shreveport, Louisiana, called Paula Records.

FRED BUDA:

You grow up, you're influenced, you go through your arrogant period—"That's great, this stinks." But then you start to realize when it's really done well, it's all great. Whether you like strawberry ice cream or not is not the issue. The fact is, strawberry ice cream is good; if you don't like it, that's okay.

CARTER BEAUFORD:

I grew from the jazz thing, then I got swept into the rock thing. I was in a group that played nothing but Beatles. It was amazing to have this little black kid playing Beatles songs. Ringo Starr was one of my heroes. I swore up and down that I was Ringo Starr.

ALEX ACUÑA:

I would put Eddie Palmieri's music on and would play along with it. I was preparing myself to become me.

DAVE WECKL:

At first, I always liked the Monkees and other pop bands. I liked Led Zeppelin and focused on John Bonham for a bit. The drummer I really got into for a minute was Jack Sperling, with Pete Fountain. I learned a lot from Jack in the early days. Then my dad turned me on to Buddy Rich with the big band thing. I was drawn to anybody who was playing with a big band. From there I got into the fusion thing.

TERRI LYNE CARRINGTON:

Keith Copeland taught me during my most formative years and really helped me develop. He taught me funk beats and Latin rhythms. Before, I had maybe just recognized reading rudiments, but Keith got me into really reading music.

While I was studying with Keith, I received a scholarship to the Berklee School of Music. I also studied piano there. Then Keith left and I started studying with a teacher there, Tony Tedesco, who was doing a lot of shows in the Boston area. He was way into the reading and technical end of things even more. After that, I studied with Alan Dawson, who I feel really polished me. Any loose ends, he tied up.

Kenny Rogers, Neil Diamond, Sawyer Brown, Lee Ann Rimes, Star Wars Soundtrack

PAUL LEIM:

By the time I was seventeen, I was making more money than my dad did. When my wife Jean and I got married as juniors in high school, I was already making a living.

Courtesy of Yamaha

Paul Leim

Carter Beauford

Photo by Jon Cohan

CARTER BEAUFORD:

I was always listening to the radio, which I loved. I would catch groups like the Beatles and the Dave Clark Five— the British rock era. Then I got into Hendrix, and at the same time I got into Tony's [Williams] Lifetime records. That's when everything took off.

The message I got from Tony was that drummers are no longer just timekeepers. We can play melodies on these tubs, we can do anything. Tony was the voice for me; he played the drums and made them sing! The ideas started flowing, and I was like, "Wow, there really are no rules here!" For years I thought jazz was jazz and rock was rock and these things weren't supposed to touch each other. Tony made me see the world with different glasses.

DAVE WECKL:

I kind of got into jazz through the back door. Once I got into Buddy, then I checked out Billy Cobham and Peter Erskine, and then I had to find out where they came from. Then I started listening to Tony and Elvin [Jones], and [Jack] DeJohnette.

ANDY NEWMARK:

I just saw a video from 1974 of me, Willie Weeks, and Ronnie Wood, and Keith Richards, and I said to Ronnie as we were watching it, "That's exactly how I play today—I don't play any different." It was really just me; nothing's changed, it just gets more refined. I'm not sure that refinement is a good thing.

CARTER BEAUFORD:

I found out I was ambidextrous by accident. My mom would smack my left hand when I picked up a fork because she didn't want me growing up to be a lefty. I saw so many drummers playing right-handed, that's the way I wanted to play, but I could play either way. I think I lead with the left a lot. That comes from trying to study certain licks. When I had the ride cymbal on the right side, I was trying to do certain licks, but they were hard for me to do. I decided to switch the kit around and totally distort things to see what would happen, what kind of sound and feel I would get, so I just took the ride cymbal and switched it to the left and came up with a different thing that felt good to me. It was an easy way to cop a new lick.

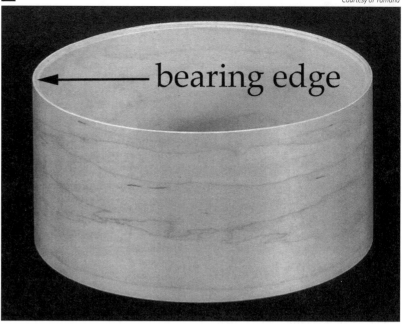

Courtesy of Yamaha

bearing edge

care And Maintenance of your Drumset

CLOSE YOUR EYES AND TRY TO IMAGINE A PERFECT WORLD

WHERE THIS IS NO DUST, NO RUST, NO GRIME. YOUR DRUMS

ARE ALREADY ASSEMBLED WHEN YOU SHOW UP AT A GIG AND

MIRACULOUSLY TAKEN DOWN AND LOVINGLY PUT IN THEIR

CASES AT THE END OF THE NIGHT BY LITTLE LEPRECHAUNS

ATTENDING TO YOUR EVERY NEED. YEAH, RIGHT! NOW WAKE

UP AND COME BACK TO PLANET EARTH. IN REAL LIFE THERE

IS WEAR AND TEAR, RUST, DUST, AND GRIME. YOU ASK A LOT

OF YOUR DRUMS, SO YOU'D BETTER NOT TURN YOUR BACK ON

THEM AND THINK THEY'LL JUST TAKE CARE OF THEMSELVES.

Think of your drumset as a finely tuned race car (I love analogies), needing cleaning, care, preventative maintenance, occasional lubrication, and rotation of the tires (stay with me here). First of all, from a practical standpoint, taking attentive care of your drums keeps them sounding and looking good. Not only can you spot problems before they develop into disasters, but by keeping an active role in servicing your kit, you extend its useful life. Drums take an awful beating (sorry), and if you are playing regularly, the abuse is compounded by the breaking down and setting up of the kit, not to mention smoke-filled clubs and rehearsal spaces, humidity, dirt, spilled beverages (usually by the lead singer), etc. Just the vibrational shock of being struck constantly can cause problems. Remember that old saying: an ounce of prevention is worth a pound of cure.

THE WELL-STOCKED DRUMMER

First, here's a short list of essential items for maintaining your drums that you should always have around.

What do you call a vibraphonist with a beeper?   An optimist.

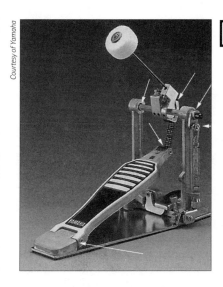

Courtesy of Yamaha

Bass Drum Pedal. Arrows indicate lubrication points

1. Drum key. An obvious one, but I've gotten to gigs and realized I've forgotten my key. A drummer friend of mine taught me to keep a key Velcro'd to the rim of the kick drum. It's easy to reach and you always know where it is.

2. Phillips and flat-head screwdrivers and Allen wrenches. These are important for removing and tightening hardware, and keeping crazed club owners at bay.

3. Very fine grade steel wool and medium or fine grit sandpaper. Steel wool is great for eliminating rust and grime from metal parts. Try it first in an inconspicuous place to make sure it doesn't scratch. Sandpaper is used to level out small inconsistencies in wood shells.

4. Graphite-based lubricant, bicycle oil, and general-purpose synthetic grease. The graphite lubricant keeps sliding metal parts like stand collars and legs dry, clean, and running smooth. Use it sparingly and keep it off any plastic parts. Bicycle or general-purpose oil works great on kick and hi-hat pedal chains. I've found general-purpose synthetic grease to be the best lubrication for tension rods and internal snare

strainer parts—anything that involves high pressure or tension.

5. Metal polish. Get a good-quality paste, liquid, or impregnated cloth, specifically designed to clean chrome and nickel. Try not to use anything with too harsh an abrasive, or it may scratch your metal.

6. Glass cleaner. Windex or any generic brand of general-purpose glass cleaner with ammonia is good for quick, light cleaning of metal parts and shells with plastic coverings.

7. Clean rags.

8. A well-lit work area with a spacious table.

9. Gig kit. I carry around a little tackle box on gigs with cymbal felts, tension rods, a bass drum beater, duct tape (the musician's best friend), snare strings or straps, hose clamps, and a hi-hat clutch. It's also a good idea to have some extra heads available in case you bust one on the gig.

Courtesy of Yamaha

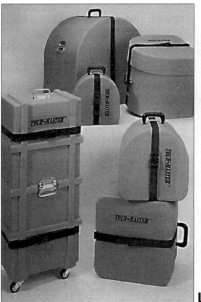

Molded plastic drum cases – "It's best to use quality cases when transporting or storing your drums."

ROUTINE MAINTENANCE
Disassembling

You need to know how your drum is put together before you take it apart to clean or repair it. While tom-toms and bass drums are fairly straightforward affairs, snare drums and stands can be a little trickier. Take a good look at the construction of the drum with the heads off before you attempt to disassemble it. Draw a diagram or keep notes, paying attention to where everything gets screwed in, put on, or fastened. There's nothing worse than stripping down a drum and meticulously cleaning every part only to realize you've forgotten how to put it back together. Have a little shoe box or tray handy to keep the small parts in.

Inspecting the Shell

The first step is to remove the drumheads by loosening the tension rods and taking the counterhoops or rims off. Check the top and bottom bearing edges of the shell to see if there are any small nicks or dents in them. If it's a wood-shell drum, you can take some medium or fine grit sandpaper to even the edges out, being careful not to over-sand the edge to the point of affecting the profile. Use a clean, wet cloth and clean off any sawdust that's left behind. Don't try fixing the shell yourself if you find any large dips or cracks in the bearing edge. Take it to a reputable drum shop that does repairs. Large shell inconsistencies, especially on bearing edges and snare beds, will not allow the head to vibrate freely on the shell and will adversely affect the drum's sound.

Remove all the lugs and metal hardware and place it to the side.

Before removing the snares from the snare drum, examine the snare string or tape to see if it is worn and needs replacing. After completely stripping the shell, take a look at it to see if there are any glaring abnormalities, like warpage or cracks. Wood shells can warp if they are exposed to a lot of moisture (e.g., a basement flood) or humidity, or if the heads are kept highly tensioned for a long period of time. One way to check for roundness is to measure the outside diameter of the drum from a few different points. If the measurements vary by more than an eighth of an inch, you probably have a drum that's out of round. Another way to check for roundness is to take a new drumhead and put it on the shell. It should go on easily and evenly. If you have to force the head onto the shell, the shell either has warped or is out of round. Neither of these scenarios is pleasant, but a good repair shop can fix some roundness problems. Unfortunately, there's not a whole lot you can do to fix a badly warped shell.

Metal Snare Drum Shells

Courtesy of Yamaha

Repairing Wood Shells

Drum shells can crack if the drums are kept in a very dry environment for extended stretches, or, if they fall off the back of a van at 65 mph. Small cracks can become big fissures, so you should try to determine the cause of the damage. A small crack in a wood drum can be fixed by applying some homemade wood filler (combine wood glue and sawdust to make a thick paste) to the inside of the shell. Don't force the filler in so hard that it will expand the crack. Let the mixture dry, reapplying if needed, then lightly sand down the repaired area.

Wood-shell drums often have some sort of polyurethane or lacquer finish, which you can clean using a sponge with a mild oil soap and water, drying the shell immediately afterwards. For more stubborn smudges and scuff marks, try some window cleaner on a clean rag. NEVER use a solvent (paint thinner, nail polish remover, etc.) on a wood shell; it will mar the finish and could possibly cause damage to the glue joints that hold the plies together.

Cleaning Chrome

Chrome-plated shells, counterhoops, and hardware can be cleaned with a good glass cleaner if they don't have too much dirt built up on the metal. Metal polish (I use a polishing paste made for automobile chrome), some super-fine grade steel wool, and elbow grease will remove heavier grime. (Some brass and bronze shells are lacquered instead of plated; in that case, use a mild soap and water for cleaning the finish.) If you really want to get serious, try cleaning the metal on a buffing wheel with some polishing rouge.

Make sure to check all the chrome for any pits or rust. Many times, you can stop the advance of pitting by cleaning the chrome with steel wool, or in extreme cases, a wire brush. Remember, rust never sleeps. Pitting and rust are caused by exposure to moisture and humidity. Store your drums in cases and keep them in a moderately dry, well-ventilated place.

Lugs, Inserts, and Tension Rods

The lug casings should be inspected for any cracks, missing parts, and stripping of the tension inserts. Take a good look at how the lug and insert are assembled so you can reassemble them correctly. I like to keep extra inserts around in case one cracks or the threads strip. You can clean out old grease and dirt from the insert using a pipe cleaner or cotton swab soaked in rubbing alcohol. Any rust or dirt on tension rods can be cleaned with steel wool, or the rod can be replaced if it's bent or stripped. Once the insert is clean, lubricate it with a small amount of general-purpose synthetic grease. The grease will allow the tension rods to thread smoothly into the insert, minimizing any chance of stripping.

How do you know when there's a drummer at your door?   His hat says "Domino's Pizza."

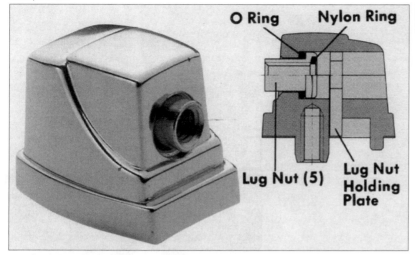

Courtesy of Yamaha

O Ring   Nylon Ring

Lug Nut (5)   Lug Nut Holding Plate

Cross section of a lug showing its different parts.

Stands and Pedals

Once you've cleaned all the shells, lugs, rims, and mounting hardware, and reassembled the drums, move on to the stands and pedals. Inspect the springs, chains, and pull rods on your hi-hat and kick drum pedals. Check for any unusual wear and tear. Stands can be tough to fix because the various components are usually attached by rivets, which cannot be unscrewed. If a rivet comes off during a gig, you can temporarily replace it with a screw and nut. Hardware has the annoying habit of breaking at the most in opportune times, like when you're onstage. If, say, the wing nut on the tightening collar of your cymbal stand strips out from being overtightened, you can use a handy-dandy hose clamp or duct tape on the stand as a stopgap measure to keep it from slipping.

Cymbals

Sure, cymbals are made of metal, but don't try cleaning them with a standard metal polish. There are many great cleaners on the market formulated especially for cymbals, and they all work well. Make sure to consult the manufacturer's recommendations before cleaning a cymbal. I try to wipe down my cymbals on a regular basis and check for cracks (see below) or any other problems. Hypothetically, if cymbals are stored and used correctly, they will last forever. Hypothetically.

Summary

As part of a regularly scheduled maintenance program (again with the automobile analogy!), you should lubricate all pedals (with bicycle oil), tension rods and strainers (with general-purpose grease), stands, mounting hardware, and thrones (with graphite lubricant and oil). Keep a record of parts you have replaced, heads you have changed, and when you have cleaned your drums. Have a small collection of replacement parts and drumheads available for quick repairs. As the Boy Scouts say, "Be prepared."

FIXING A CRACKED CYMBAL

Q. How do I fix a cracked cymbal?

A. Send it to a psychiatrist.
But seriously, folks, depending upon where the crack is located and how extensive it is, you have a few options. If the crack starts on an outer edge, cymbal expert John King of Zildjian recommends taking a stone grinding wheel and cutting a small V or U shape into the cymbal about a half an inch or so past the end of the crack. "It just takes a few seconds to do it, and it's amazing how quickly it works its way into the cymbal," says King. "A lot of the sonic qualities are still kept, as opposed to drilling or cutting the cymbal down." King advises against the popular method of drilling a small hole at either end of the crack. "The integrity of the cymbal is affected beyond the crack and what you can actually see; that's why the drilling of a cymbal usually doesn't work."

If the crack starts at the outside edge, you can try putting the cymbal on a metal lathe and cut the cymbal down in size past where the crack is. Take the cymbal to your local machine shop to see if they will do this. King says this drastically (and usually negatively) affects the sound of the cymbal.

A more extreme option that I have heard about (but never tested) is to drive epoxy deep into the cracked area, hitting the the cymbal a few times to "seat" the adhesive. Do this a couple of times, wipe away any excess, and heat the cymbal in a 200 degree (Fahrenheit) oven for an hour to cure the epoxy. Remove and serve with a garnish of chopped parsley and tomatoes.

Many stores and cymbal companies will replace cracked cymbals, depending on the situation. Most manufacturers offer a one-year replacement policy either through arrangement with the dealer or directly from the company.

Finally, a little creativity goes a long way. One drummer friend uses his severely cracked 18" crash as an effect cymbal. It sounds for all the world like a great old trashy China Boy. Work to make a disadvantage an advantage.

An excellent source book on cymbals is called, appropriately enough, The Cymbal Book, by Hugo Pinksterboer. It's available from Hal Leonard.

3:58 p.m.

Photo by Jon Cohan

A Day in The Life of Anton Fig

ANTON FIG IS THE LONG-TIME DRUMMER FOR THE DAVID

LETTERMAN SHOW. HE ALSO KEEPS BUSY WITH A SCHEDULE OF

STUDIO WORK AND LIVE GIGS. LET'S FOLLOW ANTON ON A TYPICAL

DAY AND SEE WHAT HAPPENS.

Photo by Jon Cohan

3:58 P.M.
Anton arrives at the Ed Sullivan Theater, where the Letterman show is taped. Earlier in the day he had been working on the planning of his home studio.

4:20 P.M.
The band plays "Shame, Shame, Shame" with Shepherd, while across the stage actor Danny Glover rehearses a skit against a blue screen that superimposes him dancing with Russian president Boris Yeltsin.

Photo by Jon Cohan

4:07 P.M.
Blues guitar prodigy Kenny Wayne Shepherd, a featured musical guest, arrives and meets the band. He runs through the opening theme song a few times. Anton plays uncannily difficult and different fills on each take.

4:07 p.m.

4:02 P.M.
The CBS Orchestra, cued by leader Paul Shaffer, careens through songs that will be played at commercial breaks. "Everybody's Working for the Weekend" is worked up with an actor portraying a Vegas-type lounge singer. The cues go well the first time, and the song is nailed on the second run-through by Anton and the band.

4:45 P.M.
Anton and the band rehearse more songs for the show, including "Train Kept A-Rollin" and "You Can't Judge a Book by Its Cover," a song to introduce one of the guests, a six-year-old author.

4:45 p.m.

Photo by Jon Cohan

6:30 P.M.

The show is finished. This is Friday, so there will be an extra half hour of taping for the following Monday's show. The audience stays in the theater and the band takes a fifteen-minute break before striking up the theme again.

4:55 P.M.

The band rehearses the theme song with Shepherd again and then leaves the stage.

Photo by Jon Cohan

Anton discusses postal rates with show regular Leonard Tepper

Photo by Jon Cohan

5:10 P.M.

Anton dresses and prepares for the show. The doors are opened and the audience quickly fills the theater.

5:30 P.M.

Anton and the band play the theme song and Letterman comes out to do his opening monologue.

5:20 P.M.

The band is introduced and warms up the audience with some up-tempo numbers. One of the staff writers comes out to tell some jokes.

30   *What do you call a drummer without a girlfriend?   Homeless*

The band hits at 10:30 p.m.

Photo by Jon Cohan

7:30 P.M.

Taping is finished. Anton changes clothes and quickly walks over to S.I.R. rehearsal studios four blocks away.

7:45 P.M.

S.I.R. Studio D. Anton rehearses with Jimmy Vivino, the guitarist on "Late Night with Conan O'Brien," for a record date on Saturday. The band includes Harvey Brooks on bass and session legend Al Kooper on organ.

The group prepares some blues tunes, with Anton adding thoughtful suggestions and swinging grooves to the music. The band gels almost immediately, playing the songs with feeling and soul.

Photo by Jon Cohan

Anton in full swing

9:15 P.M.

Rehearsal ends. Anton leaves for Le Bar Bat, a trendy Manhattan nightclub several blocks away. The band Anton is playing with is an original rock trio with old South African friends Keith Lentin on bass and Blondie Chaplin on guitar and vocals. Anton has just enough time to take his drums out of the road cases, set them up, and eat some dinner before hitting the stage at 10:30.

Anton, Keith, and Blondie play a mighty couple of sets before the night ends and Anton heads home after a more than full day of drumming.

Setting up his drums at Le Bar Bat

Photo by Jon Cohan

"...the drummer is always supposed to protect the rhythm, have a beat inside, protect the groove. The way you protect the groove is to have a beat in between a beat." Miles Davis

*Chick Corea,
Tania Maria,
Michel Camilo,
John Patitucci,
GRP All Star Big Band*

DAVE WECKL:

My first big gig, I would say, was in New York. It was a big gig for me because it was the catalyst for my whole career. It was getting a gig with a band called French Toast, that later became Michel Camilo's group, with Anthony Jackson playing bass at the time. Peter Erskine recommended me for the band, which came about from me bugging him to death, and sending him tapes, and him coming out and listening to a band I was in. When I knew I was gonna play with Anthony Jackson and all these other amazing musicians, I just 'shedded the music to death. I got my opportunity and came in and did the gig, so much to Anthony Jackson's liking that he recommended me for everything he was doing. At that time, I was heavily influenced by Gadd, who was one of Anthony's favorite drummers. That was the moment where, if I didn't cut that gig, you probably wouldn't be talking to me, because that was the reason that everything started to happen. Because of Anthony, I got the Simon and Garfunkel tour and a lot of studio work in town. That first important gig, the impression has to be made. You have to be ready enough to cut it.

ALEX ACUÑA:

One day Joe Zawinul called me to play percussion with Weather Report. They hired me, we rehearsed for one day, and the next day I went to Europe with them!

CARTER BEAUFORD:

We [the Dave Matthews Band] used to play in this club, Eastern Standard, that held about thirty-five people. We were playing in the window. I used a snare drum, a hi-hat, and my kick drum was the floor. The floor was hollow, so I would stomp on it. We put a mic on it and it was this awesome kick drum sound.

about drumming

Courtesy of Yamaha

Dave Weckl

Did you hear about the guitarist who bragged he could play 32nd notes?   The band didn't believe him so he proved it by playing one.

ANTON FIG:

Paul [Shaffer, bandleader on "Late Night with David Letterman"] said, "Miles Davis is coming on the show. We don't know what's gonna happen, just be prepared for anything." So I got there and there was a table with a velvet covering and a Linn 9000 drum machine. I went, "Oh, shit, they're gonna play with a drum machine!" So they said, "You're gonna play with the machine," and it sounded terrible. Then they took away the drum machine and I played. Then they said to just play with brushes, and I thought, "Oh, f**k, after brushes I'm out!"

It was Christmastime and we played "We Three Kings." It was a jazz waltz, and in the middle we just cut and Miles went into a rock thing and back into a waltz. We get through the rehearsal and everything was good. If there was anytime for me to be nervous, it was during the show. When Miles came out, I thought, "Holy shit, I'm playing with Miles Davis on TV!" And then I thought, "I'm not going to be nervous; I've worked my whole life for this." In college we listened to Miles day and night. I thought he was one of the greatest musicians of the twentieth century. So we played the song and it was fine; I felt very calm.

Afterwards I asked Marcus Miller to introduce me to Miles. My son had just been born, and Miles was asking about him. Then he said to me, "You got a good feel for them drums." And I went out of the room floating. Whenever I have a hard time on a session, or I'm not the right guy, I just say to myself, "Well, it was good enough for Miles."

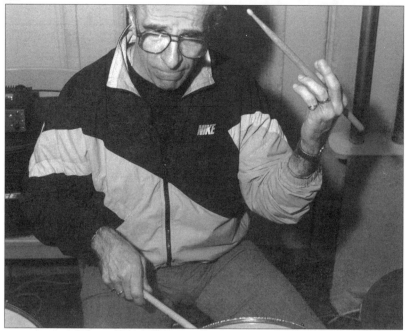

Fred Buda

Photo by Jon Cohan

FRED BUDA:

The stories with [the late Boston Pops conductor Arthur] Fiedler are legendary.... [Jazz violinist] Joe Venuti was gonna do something with the Pops, so we had a rehearsal, just the piano, bass, and drums; no orchestra. We were gonna do "Sweet Georgia Brown," and Joe just loved to hear the sidestick on the rim on the two and four. Fielder says, "What the hell is that?" I say, "It's a jazz thing," and he says, "It's not written here!" So I said, "I gotta do it for Joe, he needs that." So Fiedler says, "It confuses me!" "How does it confuse you?" He says, "I think it's on one." I say, "It's on two and four, don't worry."

The Boston Pops,
Woody Herman Band,
The Herb Pomeroy Big Band

So we get into rehearsal with the orchestra and Fiedler turns the beat around. He looks at me and says, "You're confusing me!" So I said, "Arthur, I'm gonna blink on the one and three, so you'll know where it is."

Next rehearsal I'm doing the blinking and after a while I stop, figuring he's got it. Of course he loses it! So now we get to the TV show and I start blinking on two and four and playing on one and three! Joe Venuti turns around and says to me, "You've been on this gig too long, kid!" Talk about four-way coordination—that's five-way and I blew it!

ANDY NEWMARK:

It wasn't as if I was chosen to do the John Lennon thing, the Double Fantasy album. Steve Gadd was called for that and never even got back to [producer] Jack Douglas with a yes or no. I'd say that defines being busy.

So Steve got the initial call, and they had a list of names and somehow I got the call. This is an example of where I wasn't the chosen guy, but I ended up doing it. I fell into it because someone else defaulted. If you fall into something, you've got to do it justice.

What's the difference between a harmonica and a trampoline?   You take your shoes off to jump on a trampoline.

CARTER BEAUFORD:
We played in Montreal one time and I made the mistake of changing out of my Montreal Canadians jersey into a Boston Bruins jersey for the encore 'cause I had sweated it through. Whew, man, I thought a bomb had gone off in that place! Those people went off !!

Courtesy of Yamaha

Photo by Jon Cohan

Drum Tuning 101

So you've got these great new drums. You set them up,

break out your brand-new pair of drum sticks, and get

ready to lay down the biggest groove since Moses

parted the Red Sea. Your hand drops the stick

towards the head at a dizzying speed, drum stick con-

tacts drum, and...SPLACK! THWART!!

Photo by Jon Cohan

"Wait a minute!" you say in indignant surprise, "These are the same drums that Joey Alternative played on my favorite record, 'Hurl Jam,' and they don't sound anything like his! What gives?!"

Well, Little Drummer Boy/Girl, what gives is that drums, like most other musical instruments, need to be tuned and tensioned to get the sounds you are used to hearing from your favorite drummers. The simple fact is that well-tuned drums make you sound and play better.

The way your drums sound is dependent on many different variables, including the type of material your drum shell is made of, the dimensions of the shell, the type of head you use, how you strike the head, how the batter head is tensioned in relation to the bottom head, how you muffle (or don't muffle) the drum, etc. Sure, we could talk about Chladni figures, nodal lines, and approximate pitch, but I'll just assume that you have already read Ando and Gotlob's ground-breaking 1971 scientific paper "Effects of early multiple reflections on subjective preference judgments of music sound fields." Basically, to get a great drum sound, all you need to know is this simple formula:

$$f_{mn} = (1/2\pi a)\ (T/q)\ 1/2jmn$$

What's the difference between a dead lead guitarist lying in the road and a dead squirrel lying in the road?   *There's skid marks in front of the squirrel.*

Tensioning order of a 10 lug snare drum.

Photo by Jon Cohan

Photo by Jon Cohan

For the benefit of those of you who have not received a degree in acoustical engineering or calculus, I'll try to explain in plain English:

The sound you make when you hit a drum comes from the movement of air inside the drum shell. The drumhead vibrates, air movement energy is converted to sound energy, and everybody is happy. You probably already know that a smaller-diameter drum gives you a higher pitch than a larger-diameter drum (duh!), but another important factor is the thickness of the shell. Because a thicker shell tends to dampen vibration more than a thinner shell, it has a brighter and generally higher sound. A thinner shell vibrates more easily and tends to the warmer and lower frequencies. Thicker shells are primarily more responsive at louder playing ranges, whereas thinner shells seem to operate best at lower playing volumes.

The choice of drumheads is one of the most important factors in getting your sound. Thinner, lighter heads are usually brighter and more responsive,

while thicker and plied drumheads dampen overtones and create a "wetter," fatter sound. Many rock drummers like to use a thinner head (Remo Ambassador, Aquarian Satin Finish) for the snare batter and thicker heads (Remo Pinstripe or Emperor, Attack 2, etc.) for the bass drum and tom-toms. Jazz drummers tend to go with thinner heads all around. Calfskin, which was the drum set membrane of choice before plastic heads were invented, has a warm sound and a more pliable response. Drumhead manufacturers have now come out with plastic heads that approximate the sound, look, and feel of calfskin.

CHANGING HEADS

If you're putting new heads on your drums, you must undo the tension rods and remove the old heads. Make sure that the tension rods are lightly lubricated with a good grease. This allows the rods to thread easily into the lug inserts and helps facilitate even tensioning of the head. Always check the edges and roundness of the

shell you're putting new heads on. If a shell is "out of round," the drumhead will have to be forced on and will not be able to vibrate fully and speak clearly. Also, if the bearing edges of the shell are nicked or uneven, the head will not seat properly, again causing interference with the vibration and resonance of the head. A good drum shop will have a repair department that can check bearing edges and repair any minor problems.

Take the new head and place it on the shell. I like to put the bottom head on first and establish a basic pitch for the drum. Either way, the head should be able to go on the drum without much effort. Replace the drum hoop, lining

Photo by Jon Cohan

Photo by Jon Cohan

up the ears of the rim with the corresponding lugs, and start screwing in the tension rods diagonally around the drum in the order shown in the diagram, until they are finger tight.

Once you are sure the head is seated evenly on the drum, start tightening the rods one to two turns each with a drum key in the same diagonal order. Don't be alarmed by any stretching or cracking sounds you might hear. That's just the head expanding and forming to the shape of the shell. After a couple of turns, start tapping the drumhead near its center with a stick to hear what the pitch is. Also tap around the drum, about an inch from the edge where each rod is located, to make sure the head is tuned evenly to itself. Once you've found a nice, ringing pitch, flip the drum over and start on the other head. Muffle the head you are not tuning by laying it on a towel or pillow, so you can hear the pitch of just the head you are working on. The key is to tension the head evenly on all sides, while not tightening it so much that the drum

chokes or keeping it so loose that it deadens vibrations. Brand-new drumheads often stretch even more after being tensioned initially, so you may have to make adjustments after a few minutes of playing.

SNARE DRUMS

For snare drums, I like to tension the snare-side head pretty tight and let the top head determine most of the pitch. This keeps the drum reasonably responsive, as the snares themselves are excited by the vibrations of the bottom head. It's crucial to get all the wrinkles out of the head, especially around the snare bed, because the snares will actually ride on the little rise in the head created by the bed indentation. The top head is often tensioned less than the bottom, but not always. Test different tunings to find the sound you like. If you like a fat tone, try backing off a little on both heads and leaving the snares fairly loose for a nice "spray." For that high-end crack (à la Steve Jordan), try getting both heads nice and tight and

hit the hoop along with the head in a rim shot.

To attach snares to the drum, lay the drum so the bottom head is facing up and the strainer is thrown off, then lay the snares on top of the head so they are centered on the drum. Fasten and secure the snares to the butt plate first, then to the throw-off, making sure the snares are still centered. When the snare strainer is in the up position, the snares should be allowed to vibrate easily and freely. If the snares are too tight, too loose, or not centered, make adjustments by letting out or taking in slack on the strainer itself or by loosening or tightening the snare strings or strips attached to the throw-off or butt plate.

TOM-TOMS

Many toms have an optimum tension and pitch where they seem to sound the best; with a little effort you can find that spot. One method is to get the same pitch out of both heads, so the drum is in tune with itself. To do this, find a pitch on the bottom head you are happy with, and then try to match that pitch on the top head. This procedure makes for a very resonant, ringing sound that is great for tom-toms.

Lots of drummers like to use a thinner, clear head on the bottom of their toms and a thicker, plied head on the top, which produces a pleasing timbre from the bottom head and warm, controlled overtones from the top. Again, it's well worth the time to experiment with different head and tuning combinations.

For a good sound with an even and quick decay, tune the bottom tom-tom head higher than the batter head. On floor toms, I keep the bottom head pretty loose and the top head even looser, so the wrinkles in the head are just out. This creates that great rock BOOM that engineers love. For jazz, I like to use thinner heads (like a Remo Ambassador) on the toms, tuned up to get a higher pitch and brighter attack.

BASS DRUM

I've heard 20-inch kick drums that sounded huge, and 26-inch drums that had no attack or resonance at all—go figure! Bass drums are often tuned up and stuffed with pillows or foam and never thought about again until a head breaks. This does the kick drum a great disservice, my friends. The bass drum is the soul of your kit; give it a chance to sing! Unfortunately, most sound engineers would rather have a heavily muffled bass drum, to which they can add reverb at will, because it makes their lives easier. After explaining to them that John Bonham, owner of the greatest drum sound of all time, never muffled his bass drum with anything more than some torn pieces of newspaper, let them know that you are willing to

work with them to get the best sound possible. Drumming rule #231 specifically states that under no circumstances should you ever anger a sound person; they can make your life a living hell—trust me on this one.

Realize that when you tension the batter head on a kick drum, you're going to affect the way the pedal reacts when contacting the head. A tightly tuned batter head will cause the pedal to rebound quicker than a slack head. When playing live, I tune my front head medium tight for good projection and leave the batter head looser than the front. In the studio, where I don't need the front head to be as resonant, I ease off on both heads a bit. Also, by raising the spurs on your kick drum, you elevate the front of the drum off the ground and permit it to resonate a little more.

Another technique for getting a nice full resonance out of the kick drum is to eliminate most of the muffling, using just a small felt strip placed between the front head and the shell. The strip takes just enough ring out of the drum, while still keeping warm, round tones and a fundamental pitch. This really works well if there are no microphone holes in the resonating head.

Photo by Jon Cohan

Try the old trick of putting torn paper towels or newspaper in the drum. If you have a hole in the front head, add strips of the paper a few at a time, checking the drum periodically to find the tone you like. The paper gives way to air pressure and doesn't dampen the vibrations of the head as much as foam does.

One thing I've learned as a drummer and drum tech is that it pays to be flexible. Every situation is unique—studios, stages, basements, and garages all sound different. Listen to your drums and learn how to make them sound good in any environment. Pay attention to what other drummers are doing and try to identify what makes them sound the way they do. Experiment with different combinations of tuning and heads and try to find a sound that identifies who you are as a drummer. Or, just follow the elementary formula stated earlier.

BY FRANK BRIGGS

Frank Briggs teaches drum set in the Los Angeles area, as well as through the media of books and instructional video. He has performed in clinic for Noble & Cooley, Mel Bay, Paiste, and Attack drumheads. His live and recording credits include Atlantic Starr and Mike Keneally.

Photo by Jon Cohan

The Basics of Miking Drums

THIS CHAPTER WILL DEAL WITH THE FUNDAMENTALS OF MIKING AND SUBMIXING A DRUM SET FOR LIVE PERFORMANCE AND HOME RECORDING. I NEVER MET A DRUMMER WHO DIDN'T KNOW HOW THEY WANTED THEIR DRUMS TO SOUND, AND REALLY, THAT'S AN ADVANTAGE. IT'S JUST A MATTER OF TRANSLATING THE SOUND IN YOUR HEAD TO TAPE. REMEMBER, THE BEST MICROPHONES ARE NOT GOING TO MAKE A BAD-SOUNDING DRUM SOUND GOOD; GET YOUR SOUND HAPPENING AT THE SOURCE FIRST.

Drummers can only benefit by familiarizing themselves with the different types of microphones, audio mixers, and signal processors. Look at it this way: guitarists have been dealing with this since the invention of the electric guitar. Why? It's their sound and it's important.

WHY MICROPHONES?

Talk to some guitarists and ask them what kind of pickups they use or prefer. Chances are they will be pretty specific and be able to explain why they like this or that (nice low-end crunch for leads, etc.). In fact, most guitarists will have more than one guitar, with different pickup configurations for different situations or even different songs. Why? It's their sound and it's important.

If you dropped a drummer and a drumset off a ten story building, which would hit the ground first?   Who cares!

Photo by Jon Cohan

Your microphones are your pickups, and to make things a little more complex, we need to address our drums individually. One kind of microphone will not be suitable for all your drums and cymbals (although you can mic a drum set successfully with one or two microphones...more on that later).

SELECTING MICROPHONES

The snare drum has an entirely different frequency* range from the bass drum, and the bass drum from the cymbals, the cymbals from the toms, etc. When selecting a microphone, you should choose the one that best suits the application. Don't be afraid to ask questions and make mental notes on the mics you see used over and over again. For instance, my snare drum and my tom-toms have been miked with a Shure SM57 more often than any other, both live and in the studio. This is great news for the drummer on a budget, because the SM57 sounds good and is also very affordable. If you are a real heavy hitter, you may want to consider using all dynamic* mics (* = see Glossary), as they may be better suited for high sound pressure levels, whereas condenser* mics are more sensitive. Experiment.

Snare Drum Microphones

Look for a dynamic microphone that is unidirectional* (cardioid* or supercardioid*), with a frequency response* of or around 40–16,000 Hz, that can withstand sound pressure levels of 100 dB (decibels*) or higher without distortion. Remember, a hard whack on a snare drum can reach sound pressure levels of 110 dB or higher (ear plugs, anyone?). A microphone of this type would be suitable for vocals or amplifier miking.

Tom-Tom Microphones

I personally prefer condenser mics on the toms. There are companies offering very small clip-on or clamp-on condenser microphones; these are great for a their sound quality and low profile. Dynamic mics like the Shure SM57, Sennheiser MD421U, or the

Photo by Jon Cohan

EV N/D408 also work well. Look for a microphone with a frequency response of around 40–20,000 Hz, with a cardioid or supercardioid (unidirectional) polar pattern.*

Bass Drum Microphones

Look for a dynamic supercardioid or cardioid mic with a frequency range of 20–20,000 Hz. You need this to reproduce both the very low end and the high-end click (or attack) that many drummers like. The Shure Beta 52 or a combination of the Beta 52 and Shure SM91A works well, as do the AKG D112, Neumann U47, and Sennheiser 421.

Cymbal and Overhead Microphones

To reproduce all the frequencies of your cymbals, look for a cardioid (unidirectional) condenser mic with a frequency response of 20–20,000 Hz. A typical setup would be a dedicated hi-hat mic and one overhead placed above the center of the drum set, about a foot over the drummer's head, or use two mics crossed overhead or spaced above each side of the drum set for stereo imaging. The AKG 414, KM 84, or the Shure SM81 are well suited for this task. Another option for overhead miking is to use a stereo

[Shure SM57 Mike

Photo by Jon Cohan

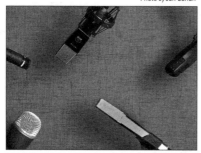
Photo by Jon Cohan

microphone for a wide spread and natural sound.

What to do when you only have...

ONE Mic: Place it in the single overhead position (see "Individual Microphone Placement and EQ").

TWO Mics: Use bass drum and overhead placement suggestions.

THREE Mics: The overhead and bass drum are still priority; place the third mic on the hi-hat facing a little towards the snare, or near the snare drum facing the hi-hat.

FOUR Mics: Experiment. Try moving the hi-hat or snare mic to cover one side and the fourth mic to pick up the floor tom side.

FIVE Mics: If you have a standard five-piece kit, keep the overhead and the bass drum mics where they are, split the third mic between the hi-hat and snare, then place a mic between the mounted toms and one on the floor tom.

SIX Mics: The hi-hat and snare can now have their own mics.

SEVEN or More Mics: Nirvana... (see "Individual Microphone Placement and EQ").

COMPACT MIXERS
What is a Mixer?

A mixer blends and colors individual sounds together. Plug all your mics into different channels* of your mixer, listen to each one separately, adjust the gain* or volume, EQ*, add reverb* or compression*, and you're on your way.

With all those buttons and knobs, a mixer can be intimidating, but in any size mixer, once you learn one channel strip you know them all. Likewise most mixers, big or small, have quite a bit in common. Learning on an eight- or sixteen-channel mixer can prepare you for a bigger console tomorrow.

Why a Personal Submixer?

With the advent of high-quality affordable compact mixers, it makes more sense than ever to own one. The applications are as varied as the benefits. I use mine for practicing; I'll run a sequencer or a play-along tape into a couple of channels along with my kit, mix it, and record my performance live to a cassette deck. Listening back will not only help you hone your chops and time, but in the process you can tweak the sound of your drums and learn how they are affected by EQ and signal processors*. I bring my mixer and microphone setup to every situation possible; I have used my rig for clinic presentations, records, and demos on a budget, as well as the audio for my instructional video. For club gigs, you don't have to be subject

to a lack of available channels on the main mixer or a lack of good mics (or no mics at all). Your sound will become much more consistent.

What to Look for in a Compact Mixer

Silence: You want a mixer that is transparent and won't add noise or hum to your sound.

Good EQ: It's very important to have nice crisp highs and clean powerful lows. Great EQ will make your cymbals sizzle and add depth and richness to your toms and bass drum.

Good Microphone Preamps: Very important.

Individual and Buss* Outs: Very handy for home recording and live submixing, a buss will allow you to combine, say, all your toms to one or two outputs. With cymbals, you could combine one stereo overhead or two overhead mics with your hi-hat mic and assign them to two channels. Individual and buss outs will allow you to mix eleven or twelve drum channels down to four, three, or even two channels. In the case of busses and individual outs, the more the better. The book entitled Mackie Compact Mixers, by Rudy Trubitt (Hal Leonard Corporation), is a great resource full of tips and suggestions. In fact, this book is a must; with all the practical applications and diagrams, you'll be mixing like a pro in no time.

 Did you hear about the guitarist who finished high school?   Me neither.

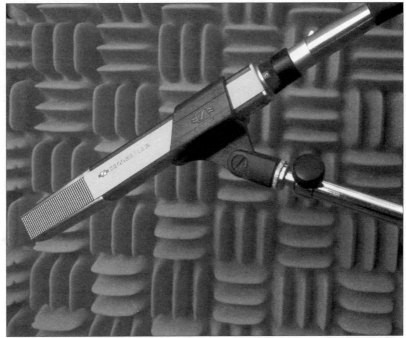

Photo by Jon Cohan

GLOSSARY

BUSS: In a mixer it is a point where individual input signals come together and are combined.

CARDIOID MICROPHONE: A unidirectional mic with a moderately wide "heart-shaped" front pickup (131 degrees). The angle of best rejection is 180 degrees from the front—i.e., directly in the rear.

CHANNEL: The controls associated with one mixer input.

COMPRESSION: Dynamic signal processing. Compression evens out the dynamic curve, guarding against loud spikes in the signal, much like a limiter.

CONDENSER MICROPHONE: A mic that generates an electrical signal when sound waves vary the spacing between two charged surfaces—the diaphragm and the backplate.

DECIBEL (dB): A number used to express output sensitivity and sound pressure levels.

DYNAMIC MICROPHONE: A mic that generates an electrical signal when sound waves cause a conductor to vibrate in a magnetic field. In a moving-coil mic, the conductor is a coil of wire attached to a diaphragm.

EQ (EQUALIZATION): Mixer controls that can change the amplitude of particular parts of

Sennheiser 421

Photo by Jon Cohan

a sound's frequency components or harmonics.

FREQUENCY: The rate at which an audio signal or object vibrates. Measured in Hertz (Hz), also called cycles per second.

FREQUENCY RESPONSE: A graph showing how a mic responds to various sound frequencies. It is a plot of electrical output (dB) vs. frequency (Hz).

GAIN: The amount by which an electronic circuit amplifies a signal. Measured in decibels.

OMNIDIRECTIONAL MICROPHONE: A mic that picks up sound equally from all directions.

POLAR PATTERN: The pickup of a microphone, plotted on a circular graph to show sensitivity in all directions.

REVERB: Within a confined space, sound can bounce back and forth repeatedly until it dies away. These reflections are called reverberations.

They can be simulated in many effects processors.

SIGNAL PROCESSORS: Also know as outboard gear, or effects processors. Reverb, delay, compression, and equalization all shape or process a signal.

SUPERCARDIOID MICROPHONE: A unidirectional mic with a tighter front pickup than a cardioid (115 degrees). The angle of best rejection is 126 degrees from the front—i.e., 54 degrees from the rear.

UNIDIRECTIONAL MICROPHONE: A mic that is most sensitive to sound coming from a single direction—in front of the mic. A cardioid mic is a unidirectional microphone.

INDIGVIDUAL MICROPHONE PLACEMENT & EQ.

	Application	Suggested Placement	EQ and Tips
BASS DRUM two heads/small hole in front head In the hole		3" to 6" away from beater head, slightly off-center from beater.	Try Boosting 60 or 100 and 2,500 Hz and rolling off (cutting) 200–500 Hz. Experiment.
			A small pillow will shorten the decay.
BASS DRUM two heads, no hole or muffling		2" to 3" away from outside head, on-axis with the beater.	Pan center, season to taste.
SNARE DRUM		Use a boom stand. Aim mic at the head, a little above the rim. Come in at an angle where the front of the mic is aimed away from the hi-hat for the best separation. A second mic may be used underneath, facing the bottom head; this will add more crack and snare sound.	Start flat; boost highs (10 kHz will help the snare cut) and sweep through the midrange until you find a sound that's natural and pleasing. Add a little reverb.
TOM TOMS		One mini condenser mounted on each drum, anywhere from 3/4 to 6 inches from batter side, just over the rim. One dynamic mic per drum or one between every two toms. Aim diaphragm at the batter head, just over the rim 1 to 2 inches.	Roll back mids, boost highs for more stick or attack, boost lows for more depth and punch. Add reverb and pan each drum according to placement.
CYMBALS (OVERHEAD)		One mono or stereo mic placed directly center, about 1 foot over the drummer's head. Two mic's placed on either side of the kit, facing down at right and left sides, or two mics crossed about 1 foot above drummer's head for stereo separation.	Roll off low end for separation from other mics. Boost highs for more sizzle. Add reverb to taste. For optimum stereo, pan mics hard left and right.
HI-HAT		Aim mic down toward the cymbals. If possible, angle away from the drummer for best separation.	Roll off lows and boost highs if necessary for more "chick" sound. Pan medium left or right.

"Mommy, I want to be a drummer when I grow up."   *"Don't be silly Johnny, you can't do both."*

Application	Tone Quality and Tips	Suggested Microphone
BASS DRUM two heads/small hole in front head In the hole	The most attack and punch. Maximum bass. Experiment with different heads: single, double, coated, clear, or heads with built-in damping. These will greatly affect the sound.	Shure Beta 52 Shure SM91A AKG D112 Sennheiser 421 Neumann U47
BASS DRUM two heads, no hole or muffling	Softer attack, very resonant sound. Great for jazz.	Two-mic combo: SM91 inside, Beta 52 6 inches from beater or outside front or batter side. Experiment.
SNARE DRUM	Should sound a lot like a snare drum. Coated single-ply head will probably work the best for most situations.	Shure SM57 or 77 Shure Beta 57A EV N/D408 Sony C-37 (tube) Two-mic combo: Beta 57A top, SM98A bottom
TOM TOMS	Natural to ambient, punchy to warm, depending on EQ and effects settings. For different tom sounds, experiment with heads. Try coated single- or uncoated double-ply for warmer sound, uncoated single-ply for brighter sound with more sustain. Experiment.	Shure SM57 Shure Beta 57 Shure SM98A Sennheiser 421 EV N/D408 Sennheiser MD504
CYMBALS (OVERHEAD)	Natural with great stereo imaging with two mics or one stereo mic. Tasteful use of reverb will add sustain and shimmer to the cymbals and ambience to the entire drum set.	AKG 414 (one or two) Shure SM81 (one or two) AKG C12 (one or two) Shure VP88 stereo mic (one)
HI-HAT	Should sound like a hi-hat. Adjust angle and height of mic for variations.	Shure SM81

Terri Lyne Carrington

Courtesy of Yamaha

about drumming

ALEX ACUÑA:

I like to search for deep players—the ones who close their eyes and their eyeballs turn white.

James Moody,
Dianne Reeves,
Herbie Hancock,
Wayne Shorter,
Danilo Perez

TERRI LYNE CARRINGTON:

All the great artists and musicians have strong personalities. They are real convinced about what they do, about life in general and music in particular. If you have the talent and have the nurturing and learn how to develop it, that really helps. Many of the musicians have their own sound and most of them are open minded. That's why you have somebody like Miles Davis, who went through so many musical phases. People like Miles, Dizzy, and Wayne Shorter are open-minded and never stop searching.

What's the difference between a podiatrist and a bad drummer?   A podiatrist bucks up your feet.

DAVE WECKL:

Sometimes for inspiration, I listen to older records that inspired me at a young age. For the real in-depth inspiration, I find it's better for me to go back, both musically and non-musically. For instance, I own a 1969 car that just inspires a certain happiness from that time period. It's the same kind of thing musically, to be able to go back and listen to my old Buddy records and watch the videos and listen to Tony Williams, or John Bonham, or even some old bootleg recording of Steve Gadd that I have from 1979 when I was nineteen and first moved to New York.

CARTER BEAUFORD:

My daughter plays drums as well. There was one day she was on her drum set and she said, "Daddy, look what I can do!" She was doing this little groove that was really weird; I couldn't figure it out because her style of playing is super unorthodox. I tried to retain this little groove. I took it home and practiced it and couldn't get it to save my life, but what came out of that is the groove for "Number 36." I have my daughter to thank for that.

ANDY NEWMARK:

I am very much inspired by other players: guys like Jim Keltner, Steve Gadd, Ricky Marrotta. I hear something and go, "Man, he has got it, he's right on that!"

TERRI LYNE CARRINGTON:

If I'm playing with somebody like Herbie Hancock, I'm very inspired because he's so inspired. He's always reaching, trying to get something. Somebody else I like playing with is Danilo Perez. He just brings something different out in me.

I feel Jack DeJohnette's influence on me stronger than any other drummer. He's a searcher. I like Elvin Jones, Roy Haynes, Tony Williams, Max Roach, all the masters. But I also listen to other styles of music.

DAVE WECKL:

It's important to realize that there's a whole history of the instrument to check out. It's not me or the Dennis Chambers or the Chad Smiths; it didn't start with us. It's a whole history of great drummers and musicians that young kids should always go back and listen to, to see where we came from. With the continued inspiration of past generations, everybody keeps moving ahead and building on what's been done already.

ANDY NEWMARK:

I try not to emulate, because that can lead you down a road where you get confused. But we are all subject to it, especially if the music lends itself to it. All of the sudden I might feel the presence of Ringo Starr. It's a very delicate line between inspiration and over-emulating.

Dave Weckl

Courtesy of Zildjian

What do you call a singer with half a brain?   Gifted.

CARTER BEAUFORD:

I'm the biggest thief on earth. I'll hear a lick and think, "That's bad!" and I'll cop it. I'll alter it a bit to add my little thing to it, so it won't be complete plagiarism. I think most musicians do that.

ALEX ACUÑA:

The book of James 1:17 says, "Every good and perfect gift comes from the Father of lights." I consider music my gift. What I play, I play for God. I'm giving the whole thing up to heaven—full joy.

TERRI LYNE CARRINGTON:

I hung out with Papa Jo Jones and Max Roach. One thing about them, they never showed me anything or gave me lessons. Just hanging out with them was a lesson. You get what you can from just talking to them.

CARTER BEAUFORD:

I went to Mickey Hart's house and we hung out together, and he showed me all these incredible drums. It just showed me that the growth process never ends. You can learn something from anybody.

"Music is about timing and getting everything in rhythm. It can sound good if it's Chinese as long as the right things are in place." – Miles Davis

BY CHRIS PARKER

Chris Parker is one of the most prolific drummers on the New York studio scene. He has recorded with such diverse artists as The Brecker Brothers, Aretha Franklin, Salt-N-Pepa, and Miles Davis, and has toured extensively with Bob Dylan. As a founding member of the legendary band Stuff, and as the house drummer for a long stint on "Saturday Night Live," his playing is a lesson in focused groove, taste, and feel. He's also clocked enough hours in the studio to know the inside of a drum booth pretty well.

Photo by Jon Cohan

Chris Parker

Lessons I've Learned In The Studio

• If possible, and believe me I know how impossible it can be, get there twenty minutes early (famous last words) to make sure your setup is the way you're comfortable with and you like it. Make sure the right drums for the date are there: your cymbals, percussion, electronics, your headphones, metronome, food, water, gaffer's tape, tools...or not.

• Make sure you have sight lines to the engineer and assistant if possible, so if you can't hear, you can at least see what he or she is doing.

Photo by Jon Cohan

- Remove your headphones immediately if you see a quizzical look on anyone's face.

- Make sure you have a route to get to the control room in a hurry. A whole conception can be lost while the producer, engineer, and other musicians are waiting for you to get out of the drum booth.

- Don't ask a lot of rhetorical questions.

- Listen.

- Read the music written for you and listen to what's on tape, or the drum loop, or the click, then use your instincts.

- Play the drums without phones on. Get them to sound good to you in the room first. Don't get a drum sound that's inappropriate for the piece or song you're about to work on.

- Don't do a chops display for the engineer or anyone else; you've already got the gig or you wouldn't be here now. Play a simple pattern or one drum at a time at a realistic playing level consistently. Again, be appropriate to the material.

- Put something on tape to listen back to critically. Are the drums sounding the way you think they should? Is the stereo imaging pleasing or where you pictured it?

- Make a comment about the sound, hopefully positive, to the engineer.

- Open your ears wide to the artist, the arranger, other players, if any, and the producer. Sometimes, a mannerism or one offhand comment will give you an insight into the tenor of the work you're about to do and the result you are expected to provide.

- Don't talk to others on mic while the arranger, producer, engineer, or artist is talking to the control room.

Photo by Jon Cohan

Chris Parker

Photo by Jon Cohan

- Remember your first instincts for the tune; even notate what you played if possible. Also, take a metronome reading of the rundown and first take—double check it on playback and note the tempo for future reference. Many, many times, after numerous takes, someone will want to get back to that first rundown tempo or feel from two hours ago, and it's up to you to recreate the groove authentically.

- Be open to suggestions and directions, but remember, you are playing the drums; your part has got to work for you—believe in it even though you may alter the dynamics, the density, and the tempo.

- Defy isolationism – don't be a prisoner of the drum booth. Make sure you can hear everything that's being said, not just what relates to the music and the arrangement, or only what pertains to the drum part.

- Tune the drums to the song. Pick common tones like the dominant for the bass drum and use regular intervals like fourths for the tom-toms.

- Get used to hearing the drums deep in the mix. Don't go nuts looking to hear the little hi-hat stuff you're doing way up front in the mix.

- Play the song.

Blues singer's tombstone reads: *"I didn't wake up this morning."*

"The growth process never ends. You can learn something from anybody." – Carter Beauford

Photo by Jon Cohan

Photo by Jon Cohan

- Pace yourself to give your best performance every take. Everyone else can punch in; you can too if you're good. (Hint: don't let the cymbals bleed.)

- Don't be offended when someone looking to make a comment starts with, "What if the drums are playing such and such...." I call comments like this "what ifs." It's best to try these suggestions and be cooperative, but use your instincts and serve the music.

- Try not to have any preconceived notions about the artist, the music, the engineer, the studio, or the producer. Have an open mind.

- I think the most important concept is having the widest range of listening experiences and the retention of stylistic signatures not only of other drummers, but also of as many different types of music and the periods in which they were played.

Courtesy of John Aldridge

some Handy Grooves

Hey kiddies, here's a few basic beats that you might be called upon to play at one time or another in the course of your drumming career. There's not many things more embarrassing than not knowing what to play when the band leader calls out a bossa nova at a gig. It's important to familiarize yourself with as many different types of music as you can. Try to get inside of the different styles and understand what's going on rhythmically. It not only opens up further opportunities to play, it also helps to make you a well-rounded musician.

These grooves are starting points for further explorations into the different styles of music. Of course not all rock music is *boom smack, boom boom smack,* just as not all jazz drumming is *ching chinga ching chinga ching chinga ching.* Have some fun with the beats - mix and match accents, placements, and tempos when you practice them. Take the shuffle for example: try throwing in different accents and fills to move the beat along.

Listen to how your favorite drummers imprint standard grooves with their own personality. Everybody has a different take on feel and swing. You can also check out some the the Essential Drum Books listed in the back of this book to further explore your options as a drummer.

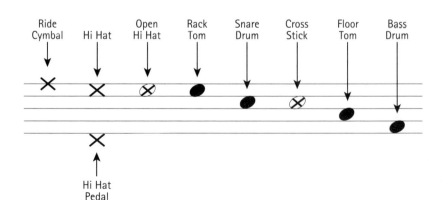

What's the definition of a gentleman?   One who knows how to play the drums, but doesn't.

1. JAZZ TIME

This is the building block that most jazz is framed upon. Swing the broken triplets and play around with where you place them. True swing music usually has a four on the floor pattern, that is, four bass drum quarter notes quietly keeping the pulse. You can also use rim clicks instead of snare hits for softer music. Though it's a deceptively simple beat, jazz time can contain many nuances that, when played properly, is a great launching pad for some exciting drumming.

2. JAZZ WALTZ

Here's just one of many variations of an approach to a jazz waltz. Brushes can be used, as can rim clicks, or mallets. Try to mix up the hi hat pedal on the second and third beat. Both the jazz time and waltz beats are great bedrocks to practice independence and coordination over.

3. SHUFFLE

The shuffle looks easy enough at first, but can take a lifetime to master the swing and feel properly. It's one of those grooves that is used in jazz, rock, country music, the blues, etc. Just in blues music alone, there are as countless variations on the shuffle. Some drummers like to keep a quarter note bass drum pulse going while swinging the cymbal and varying the accent on the snare drum. I've even heard drummers play eighth note triplets on the snare drum all the way through and accenting the two and four heavily. Interestingly enough, a lot of rock drummers have a hard time playing a shuffle, probably because the broken triplet isn't as prevalent as the straight eighth note feel.

In this example, I put ghost notes on the *and* of the *one* and *three*. You can move these to the *and* of the *two* and *four* or just drop them all together. It doesn't really matter, just make it swing.

4. ROCK

This simple beat is one of the first rhythms many of us learn on the drum kit. It's the basis for the straight eighth note feel both in rock and rhythm and blues. By accenting the *and* of the *four* on the hi hat, it becomes a little funkier. By alternately adding and excluding bass drum bombs, it becomes heavier. You can even mess with the hi hat pattern to push the feel along. Have fun and play loud!

How many lead guitarists does it take to change a lightbulb?   *None.*   *They just steal somebody else's light.*

5. FUNK BOMB

Not too different in character from the rock beat, this groove underscores the importance of what James Brown called "The One." The theory behind behind shaking is that, by stressing the bass drum hit (along with the electric bass) on the first beat of every measure or two, you create an impact that makes it almost physically impossible for people not to dance. The little sixteenth note anticipations on the kick just serve to highlight the note that follows. Scramble some ghost notes on the snare, swing the hi hat, syncopate the kick, and you're getting pretty close to hip hop my friends.

6. OLD SCHOOL FUNK

Another "rule" of funk is to drop hits where people expect them, only to have them crop up somewhere else. The anticipation of the beat drives the kids wild, I'll tell you! This two bar groove is a classic example of the syncopated style of funk that James Brown practically invented. Careers have been built on different variations of this rhythm and thanks to the wonders of modern digital sampling technology, this type of groove will probably never go out of style. As Funkateer George Clinton once said, "Funk not only moves, it removes."

7. THE ONE DROP

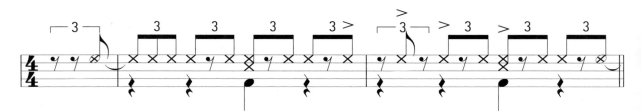

These two essential reggae beats come from drummer and music educator Rick Roccapriore. Where rock beats generally hit the snare on the two and four, reggae is all about the one and three. It's almost as if reggae is a backward rock beat. The One Drop is an exercise in funky reggae grooving, where the bass drum and rim clicks fall in the holes where the guitar drops out. Listen to Bob Marley's aptly titled song "One Drop" for a good example of this beat.

8. FOUR ON THE FLOOR

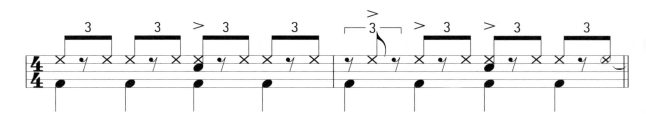

This is the more aggressive of the reggae beats, with the bass drum keeping a constant quarter note pulse and the hi hat accents making the song move along. Irie!

 Why was the piano invented? So musicians would have a place to put their beer.

9. SECOND LINE

This classic New Orleans street beat is adapted for the drum set. The Second Line grew from a mixture of marching cadences, and West African and West Indian rhythms. The kick drum pattern can stay the same while alternating flams and accents on the snare. Try keeping a quarter note pattern on the hi hat pedal.

10. BOSSA NOVA

11. SAMBA

Two classic rhythms from the incredibly deep well of Brazilian music. Samba is the older of the two grooves and more evidently reflects it's African influence. It can be propulsive and lilting at the same time. The Bossa Nova is silky and artful, with the clavé implied more often than not.

DAVE WECKL:
I think the drummer is the key to making any band click. The drums are the foundation, the dynamic, the feel, the pulse, everything.

TERRI LYNE CARRINGTON:
There's a lot of weight on the drummer. You can control the dynamics and overall feeling of the music.

PAUL LEIM:
Knowing what's going on and hopefully what's coming next is very important.

 What's the difference between a drum machine and a drummer?   A drum machine won't sleep with your girlfriend.

FRED BUDA:

The first day I ask all my students a question: How do you phrase music? All music is phrased. As a drummer, the way you can phrase music is by playing louder or softer and that includes accents. That's your strongest tool. I make them listen to Mel Lewis, who was a master at dynamics and color and taste and didn't have a lot of hands. That's what everybody thinks about—hands, hands, hands. Drummers can get so into chops. But the guys that get the gigs are the guys that are grooving. They make the other players want to bring themselves to the table and play.

ALEX ACUÑA:

That's all it is really, is to be able to understand rhythms, to be able to hear and play them, for the flavor. You know, there are people who only like to eat hamburgers. There are people who only like to eat rice and beans. Sometimes I like to eat hamburgers and rice and beans.

PETER ERSKINE:

Time keeping is the most basic fundamental. Beyond that, a drummer should play in such a way as to allow the other musicians he or she is working with to create as opposed to correct the music.

Fred Buda

Courtesy of Yamaha

Courtesy of Yamaha

TERRI LYNE CARRINGTON:

What I think about is the groove, the overall feel. Whether it's avant-garde or pop, I try to think how it feels. If it feels good, I kind of get caught up in it. Once the flow happens, it just seems real natural.

*The Late Show,
Ace Frehley,
Spider,
Joan Armatrading,
Gary Moore,
Paul Butterfield*

ANTON FIG:

Make sure the music comes first. Whatever you do should serve the song. Take care of the time, and make sure it feels good. To me time is like metronomic time. If you add the human emotion into that, you get feel. Time plus heartbeat equals feel. The important thing when you sit down and play drums is to go for the feel. I feel like the drummer is almost the shepherd, and their responsibility is to make sure everyone is in the same place, time-wise. Like Miles Davis said, "Protect the beat." You're the guardian of the beat.

CARTER BEAUFORD:

I think that's where it all comes from—studying all different kinds of music and drummers, from country to African drummers. Trying to put upstairs in the head what's happening in the world and not to be blind to what the real deal is.

PETER ERSKINE:

Music can reach across all boundaries of race, geography, and even time. Music is sound and rhythm and logic and architecture and mathematics and chaos and passion and want; reverence, irreverence, love, and sometimes hate. Music is life—we should try to show as much love and care with our music as we would in life. That means an aesthetic ideal, coupled with patience and respect, articulated with clarity and delivered with sincerity.

ALEX ACUÑA:

If I want to go to Cuba, I want to be able to play with Cuban musicians. If I go to Brazil, I want to be able to play with Brazilian musicians. I come to the United States, I want to be able to play with the American musicians. I get inside the style.

Saturday Night Live, Donald Fagen, Bob Dylan, Natalie Cole, Aretha Franklin, Stuff, Brecker Brothers, Quincy Jones

CHRIS PARKER:

Musicology is very important—perhaps the broadest possible knowledge of musical styles: regional, ethnic, international, religious, operatic, classical, modern, etc. A descriptive vocabulary is always helpful. People must communicate to make good music.

Courtesy of Yamaha

Chris Parker

DAVE WECKL:

Knowledge is the key to everything, and the more knowledge you have of past and present musics, the more well-rounded musician you will be yourself.

ANTON FIG:

It was funny, but I saw jazz as a way to make myself a better rock player. In all these different styles of music, you've got to take care of the feel. So if you go for the feel, and you take time to study the music and learn all the different nuances, you can make it work. It's not such a major stretch from one style to another.

PAUL LEIM:

I do not see myself as only a "country" drummer. I was on the road with Tom Jones, Neil Diamond. I recorded with Lionel Richie. I did Star Wars with John Williams. To me it's being able to perform music, it's being able to play the right thing at the right time, or not play anything at all if that's what is needed.

Courtesy of Yamaha

Anton Fig

What's the range of a clarinet?   *Thirty yards if you have a good arm.*

Courtesy of Yamaha

A young Terri Lyne Carrington

TERRI LYNE CARRINGTON:

Keep an open mind and listen to as many different styles of music as possible. You can learn something from every and any drummer. Take it all in and try to be versatile.

ALEX ACUÑA:

If you understand African music, you will understand Brazilian music and Cuban music. And if you study Indian music, the odd times and the tablas, you will understand almost everything.

FRED BUDA:

An orchestra responds to the baton, but they also respond to sound. It's like you're the second conductor. You've got to find the middle ground. It's so big, so many different churches of where they think the time is. Many times what I'll do is make them listen for the time.

ANDY NEWMARK:

You need good time, feel, the ability to listen, being able to connect all the players in the band together, being the common denominator of all the things going on. You've got to hear the drums as a voice or a point of view.

Courtesy of Yamaha

Andy Newmark

CARTER BEAUFORD:

With the Matthews band I get to play pretty much whatever I want, within reason. It needs to groove, to make people move and get up. You want to shake them up, but not all night.

ANDY NEWMARK:

If the music is happening, if you're involved in the moment, it makes you feel great. If I enjoy the players and the music, it doesn't matter what side of the bed I got up on.

What's the difference between a club owner and a sperm?   *The sperm has a one in a million chance of becoming a human being.*

DAVE WECKL:

To me, what makes a great musician, and I'm kind of using Buddy Rich's words here, but it hit me so hard when I heard him say it: It's not so much the technical prowess that really impresses people. What really hits them in the heart is the emotion that they can evoke out of the listener. How much of themselves can the musician put out there. As Buddy said, the ones who figure out how to evoke the most emotion, win. There's a sensitivity factor that I've noticed in the great musicians. Just that little touch of genius, something special, an ability to communicate through emotion.

ANDY NEWMARK:

I can really dissect the simplest thing and get into "Was the dynamic on the hi-hat right?" I don't mind that. If you're aware of those subtleties and can access that, then you can bring about changes in your playing for the better.

Weather Report,
Steely Dan,
Stan Kenton,
Steps Ahead,
Joni Mitchell,
Joe Henderson,
Maynard Ferguson,
Bass Desires

PETER ERSKINE:

I hope to always play for the music. If that means it swings or feels good, then excellent. I try to play the drums using space, dynamics, and a good touch. If I don't enjoy listening to what I've done, then I can't expect others to.

Peter Erskine

Courtesy of Yamaha

ANTON FIG:

I don't want to play the same part on the theme song all the time, so I'll try different stuff even if it doesn't work and try and expand on the stuff I know I can do. I like all styles of music. It would be terrible to be playing the same thing all the time. If you're in a big touring band, you can get the tempos perfect and get really deep inside the songs. That's really nice. Here [the Letterman show] we don't have a chance, it's completely different every day. You've got to make it sound seamless.

FRED BUDA:

When I was with Woody [Herman], I used to play too loud and too many notes. Woody didn't talk to anyone until he was sure you'd be okay for the band. After two nights he didn't say anything to me. So I said, "Is everything okay, Mr. Herman?" He says, "Yeah, kid, it's okay. But you know that break in 'Apple Honey'?" I says, "Yeah." He said, "I don't want to hear everything you ever learned!"

TERRI LYNE CARRINGTON:

You don't get everything from just practicing. After a while it becomes clear what you should work on. You can't practice an open mind.

What's the difference between a booking agent and a sack of manure?   The sack.

DAVE WECKL:

I think you figure out pretty quickly when you're young if you have a talent for something. Human nature is such that if we see rewards for hard work, it's inspiring to continue to do more hard work even better. If it's something that comes to you pretty easily, I guess that's what constitutes natural ability or innate talent. It doesn't mean you're gonna be great at anything without spending a great deal of time making it part of your natural being and working at it.

PAUL LEIM:

You've got to play every time you get the chance, even if it's for free. You've got to listen to every piece of music you can get your hands on. And you have to be willing to work your way up from the bottom, just like all the rest of us did. You've got to be dedicated. You have to intensely love it, and you've got to do it because you love it and not because of the money.

ANDY NEWMARK:

I'm always editing myself. Sometimes I like what I did, sometimes I think I know a better way. If that situation comes around again, I'll make a mental note not to do something a certain way. For a few years my perception will be one thing, and a couple of years later the same thing might be approached differently.

Alex Acuña

Courtesy of Yamaha

Photo by Jon Cohan

Fred Buda

ANTON FIG:

I'm constantly re-looking at myself and trying to improve. I know when I'm on top of my game and when I'm not. It's never a question of ego for me; I'm pretty realistic about what I can and cannot do. All you've got to do is go out and listen to what other drummers can do and you get a quick reality check.

TERRI LYNE CARRINGTON:

Fifty percent of drumming is mental. If you don't have the mental aspects down, it doesn't matter how much technique you have, it's not gonna mean anything without your mind at work just as hard.

PETER ERSKINE:

Years ago, when I was in the group Weather Report, Jaco Pastorius once said to me, "Hey, man, ...don't think so much when you play; just CONCENTRATE."

70 *What's the difference between mutual funds and musicians?   Mutual funds mature and make money.*

ANDY NEWMARK:

You can have both. You can think and analyze and dissect every little nuance, but still reserve a part of your brain to have emotional content.

DAVE WECKL:

I try to have the sensitivity to know how to approach both dynamically and musically the music I'm playing. Having the technique to do what a lot of people can't do is great, but the key is to do it with feeling and emotion and hopefully make it musical.

PAUL LEIM:

The reason they call me is because they want what it is I do. Fifteen years ago they'd call me because somebody else couldn't make it. Now guys get called cause I can't make it.

PETER ERSKINE:

After all is said and done, I think that acoustic music-making will remain the best way to realize music. The limits and boundaries of drumming possibilities have been getting a good stretching in the last few years (technically and style-wise). More and more musics of the world will be incorporated into drum set playing (as manifested not only by beats per se, but also by technique, i.e., drummers playing "clave" patterns with their left foot while doing all sorts of other stuff on the kit.... "In my time," we were worried pretty much with just playing the hi-hat on beats two and four!). It's always going to get better, and it will never be as good as much that's come before.

FRED BUDA:

There's only one of you. Especially playing the drums. It's the only instrument on this stage that's American and is still evolving.

ALEX ACUÑA:

Just as I have an accent speaking English, there is an accent that is my sound, that is my voice in every music that I play.

DAVE WECKL:

My goal is to stay healthy enough to be able to do what I do, the way I want to do it, for as long as I can. If I can achieve that, I'll be happy. When I look at tapes of guys like Buddy or Elvin, or Roy Haynes, I hope to be walking by the time I'm that age, much less playing drums.

Peter Erskine

Photo by Jon Cohan

Why do guitarists put drumsticks on the dash of their car?   *So they can park in the handicapped spot.*

Photo by Jon Cohan

Young street drummer in New Orleans

PAUL LEIM:

I keep myself fresh because I know how lucky I am. There's no other thing on the planet that I'm prepared intelligently enough to do to make the kind of living I make. You think that doesn't scare me? If they quit calling me, I'm in a heap of hurt!

ANDY NEWMARK:

For every good project that I'm involved in, there are also periods of unemployment. It's not one glamorous gig after another. I've been lucky to survive this long. I sometimes think this could all end tomorrow, but I've had a great run at it. Been very lucky, met many of my idols. I've been able to make a contribution to the overall picture.

ANTON FIG:

I'm getting older and I'm starting to think, "Well, this is what I can do and can't do." And let me not anguish over what I can't do; let me strive for it, but let me enjoy what I can do. It's getting more fun to play.

FRED BUDA:

Having the gift, having the talent and the luck is not gonna keep the gig. You gotta keep up, do the work. There's always some whippersnapper writing a lick trying to see if you can play it. In this business you learn till the day they put the wooden suit on you.

drum rudiments

Drum rudiments are an integral part of the education of any serious drummer. Even if you don't plan on becoming part of a drum corps or a symphonies percussion section, the rudiments are a great way to help develop hand coordination, independence and endurance. They also help to build and condition the muscles in your hands that help you control dynamics and touch. The forty rudiments notated here are the internationally acknowledged exercises developed by the Percussive Arts Society. The PAS has played a major role in standardizing and formulating the rudiments up from the original thirteen rudiments defined in the 1930's.

If you are a beginning drummer, seek out a reputable instructor who will explain the proper method of holding your sticks and playing the rudiments correctly. Use a metronome when practicing, starting at a comfortable tempo. As your ability increases, speed up the tempo and change your dynamics often. Don't be fooled by silly names like pataflafla and ratamacue; mastering some of these babies is really hard work, but definitely worth aiming for. Remember the old adage, "No Inverted Flam Tap, No Gain."

Why are the hearts of booking agents so highly coveted for transplant?   *They've had so little use.*

PERCUSSIVE ARTS SOCIETY INTERNATIONAL DRUM RUDIMENTS

All rudiments should be practiced: open (slow) to close (fast) to open (slow) and/or at an even moderate march tempo.

I. ROLL RUDIMENTS

A. SINGLE STROKE ROLL RUDIMENTS

1. SINGLE STROKE ROLL*

2. SINGLE STROKE FOUR

3. SINGLE STROKE SEVEN

B. MULTIPLE BOUNCE ROLL RUDIMENTS

4. MULTIPLE BOUNCE ROLL

5. TRIPLE STROKE ROLL

C. DOUBLE STROKE OPEN ROLL RUDIMENTS

6. DOUBLE STROKE OPEN ROLL*

7. FIVE STROKE ROLL*

8. SIX STROKE ROLL

9. SEVEN STROKE ROLL*

10. NINE STROKE ROLL*

11. TEN STROKE ROLL*

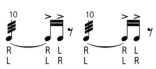

12. ELEVEN STROKE ROLL*

13. THIRTEEN STROKE ROLL*

14. FIFTEEN STROKE ROLL*

15. SEVENTEEN STROKE ROLL

II. DIDDLE RUDIMENTS

16. SINGLE PARADIDDLE*

17. DOUBLE PARADIDDLE*

18. TRIPLE PARADIDDLE

19. SINGLE PARADIDDLE-DIDDLE

III. FLAM RUDIMENTS

20. FLAM*
L R   R L

21. FLAM ACCENT*

L R L R R L R L

22. FLAM TAP*

L R R L L L R R L L

23. FLAMACUE*

L R L R L L R
R L R L R R L

24. FLAM PARADIDDLE*

L R L R R R L R L L

25. SINGLE FLAMMED MILL
L R R L R R L L R L

26. FLAM PARADIDDLE-DIDDLE*
L R L R R L L L R L R L L R R

27. PATAFLAFLA
L R L R R L L R L R R L

28. SWISS ARMY TRIPLET
L R R L L R R L
R L L R R L L R

29. INVERTED FLAM TAP
L R L R L R L R L R

30. FLAM DRAG

L R L L L R L R R L

(26. continued)

IV. DRAG RUDIMENTS

31. DRAG*

L L R   R R L

32. SINGLE DRAG TAP*

L L R L R R L R

33. DOUBLE DRAG TAP*

L L R L L R L R R L R R L R

34. LESSON 25*

L L R L R L L R L R
R R L R L R R L R L

35. SINGLE DRAGADIDDLE
R R L R R L L R L L

36. DRAG PARADIDDLE #1*

R L L R L R R L R R L R L L

37. DRAG PARADIDDLE #2*

R L L R L L R L R R L R R L R R L R L L

38. SINGLE RATAMACUE*

L L R L R L R R L R L R

39. DOUBLE RATAMACUE*
L L R L L R L R L R R L R R L R L R

40. TRIPLE RATAMACUE*

L L R L L R L L R L R L R R L R R L R R L R L R

A recording of the International Drum Rudiments as performed by Rob Carson, the three-time WORLD SNARE DRUM CHAMPION, is available from Alfred Publishing Co., Inc.

Here are some other great drum related books, both instructional and informational, that are distributed by Hal Leonard. Most music stores will stock these.

Chart Reading Workbook for Drummers
(00659129)
Bobby Gabriele

The Complete Drumset Rudiments
(06620016)
Peter Magadini

Creative Timekeeping
(06621764)
Rick Mattingly

Cross-Sticking Studies
(00330377)
Ron Spagnardi

The Cymbal Book
(06621763)
Hugo Pinksterboer

Drum Concepts & Techniques
(00604953)
Peter Erskine

The Drum Perspective
(06620015)
Peter Erskine

Drum Techniques
(06620014)
Vernel Fournier

Drum Wisdom
(06630510)
Bob Moses

The Drumset Musician
(06620011)
Rod Morgenstein & Rick Mattingly

Master Studies
(06631474)
Joe Morello

Modern School for Snare Drum
(00347777)
Morris Goldenberg

Musician's Guide to Polyrhythms
(06620613)
Peter Magadini

The New Breed
(06631619)
Gary Chester

Progressive Independence
(00330290)
Ron Spagnardi

Star Sets: Drum Kits of the Great Drummers
(00330113)
Jon Cohan

When In Doubt, Roll
(06630298)
Bill Bruford

Working the Inner Clock
(00695127)
Phil Maturano